T0343035

Cambridge Little Steps 2

Numeracy Book

Lorena Peimbert

Cambridge Little Steps 2

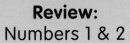

1 **Numbers 1 to 5**

◯ Trace. 2¹₃ Count. ✎ Draw.

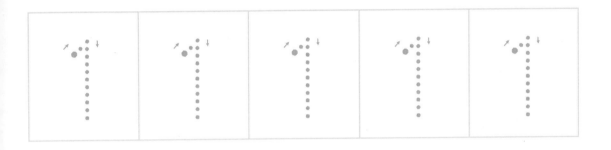

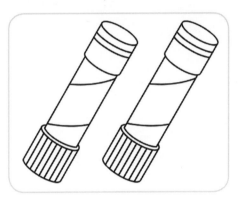

Presentation: Make a set of cards with one or two drawings of the same school object on each card. Show children a card. Ask: *What's this? (A paintbrush.) How many [paintbrushes] can you see?* Children count and say. Finally, children open their books and trace the numbers. Then they draw lines from each set of numbers to the corresponding number of school objects.

Practice: Give children a white sheet of paper and different colored pencils. Put the cards you made inside a bag. Play some music and have children pass around the bag. Stop the music. The child with the bag pulls out a card, shows it to the class, and counts the school objects on it. Each child writes the number (1 or 2) on their sheet of paper using the colored pencil of their choice. Repeat as many times as you wish.

○ Trace. 2^1_3 Count. ✏ Color.

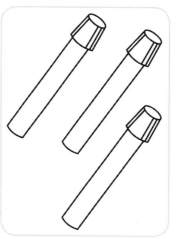

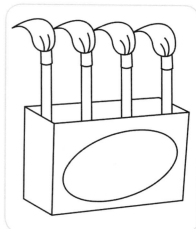

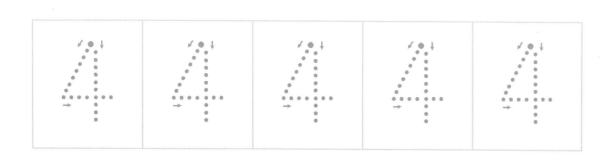

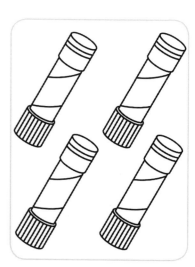

Presentation: *Make a set of cards with three or four drawings of the same school object on each card (pencil, marker, scissors, glue stick, paintbrush). Show children a card. Ask: What's this? (A marker.) How many [markers] can you see?* Children count and say. Finally, children open their books and trace the numbers. Then they count and color the corresponding number of school objects.

Practice: Display the cards facing the board at a height children can reach. Children go to the board and turn over a card. Then they count the pictures and write the correct number on the board. Repeat as many times as you wish.

◯ Trace. 2¹₃ Count. ◯ Circle.

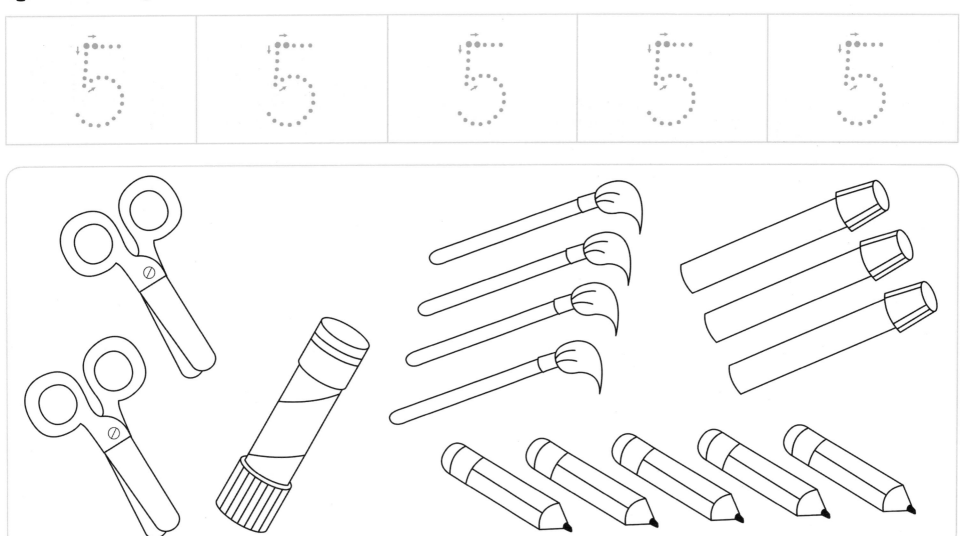

Presentation: Make a set of cards with five drawings of the same school object on each card (pencil, marker, scissors, glue stick, paintbrush). Show children a card: Ask: *What's this? (A pencil.)* *How many [pencils] can you see?* Children count and say. Finally, children open their books and trace the numbers. Then they count to find the five objects that are the same and circle them.
Practice: Toss a ball to a child. The child says *one* and tosses the ball to another child, who says *two*. Continue until a child says *five*. That child goes to the board and writes the number 5. Repeat as many times as you wish.

5

2¹₃ Count. ◯ Trace.

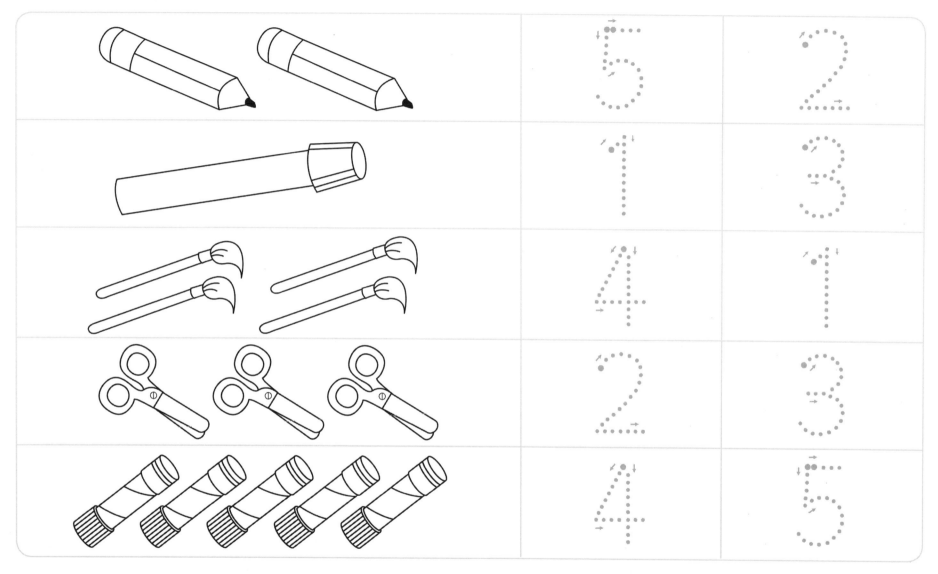

Presentation: Make a set of cards with one to five drawings of the same school object on each card (pencil, marker, scissors, glue stick, paintbrush). Show children a card. Ask: *What's this? How many [glue sticks] can you see?* Children count and say. Finally, children open their books, count each set of school objects, and trace the correct number.

Practice: Display the cards on the board. Two children go to the back of the classroom. Say: *Touch three!* Children walk fast to the board and touch a card with three school objects. Repeat as many times as you wish.

Numbers 6 to 10

2$\frac{1}{3}$ Count. ⬭ Trace. ✏ Draw.

7

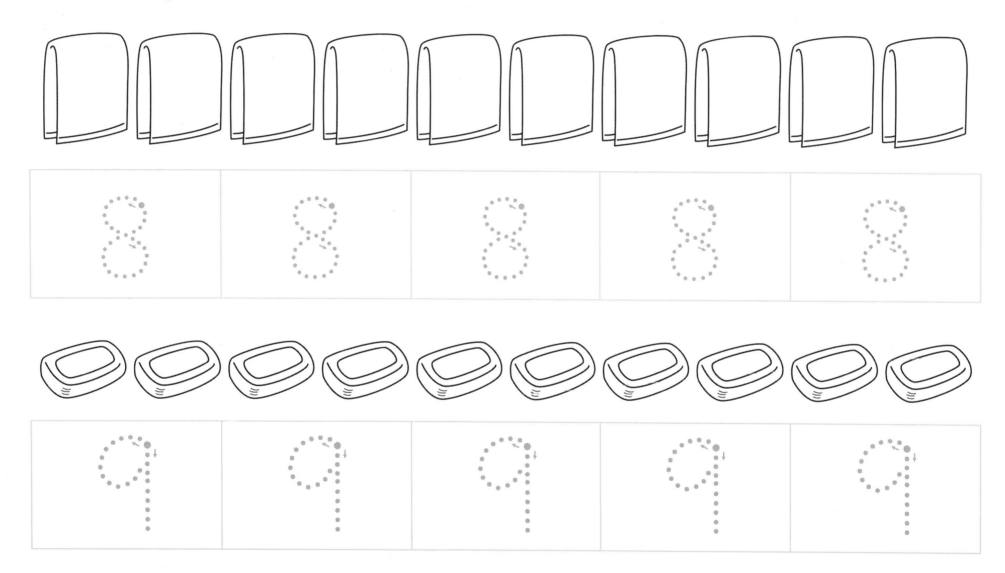

2¹₃ Count. ◯ Trace. ✏ Color.

Presentation: Make a set of cards with eight or nine drawings of the same object we use to take care of our bodies on each card (towel, soap, toothbrush, brush, jump rope). Show children a card. Ask: *What's this? How many [towels] can you see?* Children count and say. Finally, children open their books. Have them trace the number 8s and color in eight towels. Then have them trace the number 9s and color in nine bars of soap.

Practice: Display the cards around the classroom. Invite various children to the board. Say: *Find and write eight!* Children look for a card with eight objects, attach it to the board, and write the number 8 below it. Do the same for number 9. Repeat until all children have participated.

✏️ Draw. **2¹₃** Count. ⭕ Trace.

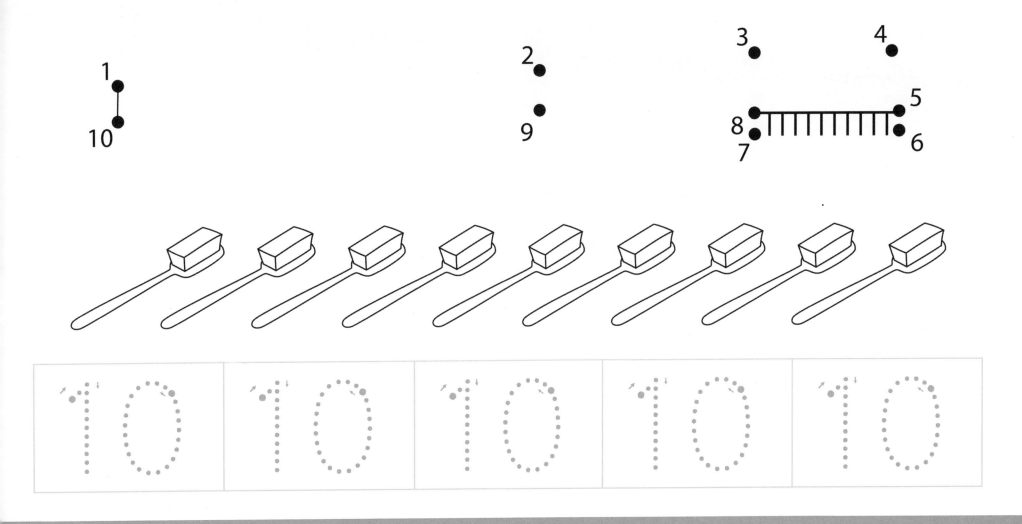

Presentation: Make a set of cards with ten drawings of the same object we use to take care of our bodies on each card (towel, soap, toothbrush, brush, jump rope). Show children a card. Ask: *What's this? How many [brushes] can you see?* Children count and say. Children open their books. Have them count and draw a line to connect the ten dots that make up the big toothbrush. Then have them count the toothbrushes and color them in. Finally, children trace the number 10s.

Practice: Children sit in a circle. Give a child a ball. That child says *one* and passes the ball to a child next to him or her. That child says *two* and passes the ball. Children continue in this manner until they reach *ten*. Lead children in counting to ten. Then have children turn to a classmate and trace the number 10 on his or her back.

²₃¹ Count. 🔲 Say. ⭕ Trace.

Presentation: *Make a set of cards with one to ten drawings of the same object we use to take care of our bodies on each card (towel, soap, toothbrush, brush, jump rope). Show children a card. Ask:* What's this? How many [toothbrushes] can you see? *Children count and say. Finally, children open their books, count the bubbles, and trace the numbers.*

Practice: *Make a set of cards with numbers from 1 to 10 and put them in a bag. Display the cards with one to ten objects on the board. Play music as children pass around the bag. When you stop the music, the child with the bag pulls out a number and puts it below the card with the corresponding number of objects on the board. Repeat until all numbers have been pulled from the bag.*

3 Numbers 11 to 13

$2\frac{1}{3}$ Count. ✏ Color. ⭕ Trace.

Presentation: Make a set of cards with eleven objects we can find at home on each card (lamp, bed, fridge, sofa, shower). Show children a card. Ask: *What's this? How many [sofas] can you see?* Children count and say. They open their books. They count the lamps and color in the number 11. Finally, children trace the number 11s.

Practice: Display various cards with numbers 1 to 11 around the classroom. Create at least five cards with number 11. Play some music and encourage children to dance to the rhythm. Stop the music and say: *Touch number eleven!* Children walk quickly to touch the correct card. They stay still until you play the music again. Repeat as many times as you wish.

2¹₃ Count. ✏ Color. ⭕ Trace.

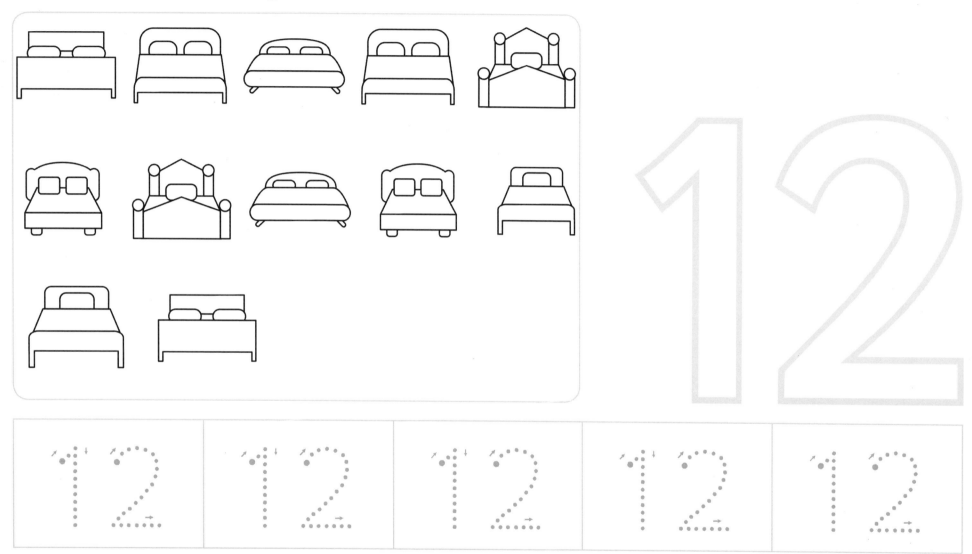

Presentation: Make a set of cards with twelve objects we can find at home on each card (lamp, bed, fridge, sofa, shower). Show children a card. Ask: *What's this? How many [lamps] can you see?* Children count and say. Children open their books. They count the beds and color in the number 12. Finally, children trace the number 12s.

Practice: Put the cards in a bag. Play some music as children pass around the bag. Stop the music. The child with the bag pulls out a card, shows it to his or her classmates, and counts the objects as he or she claps. Repeat as many times as you wish.

2¹₃ Count. ✏ Color. ⭕ Trace.

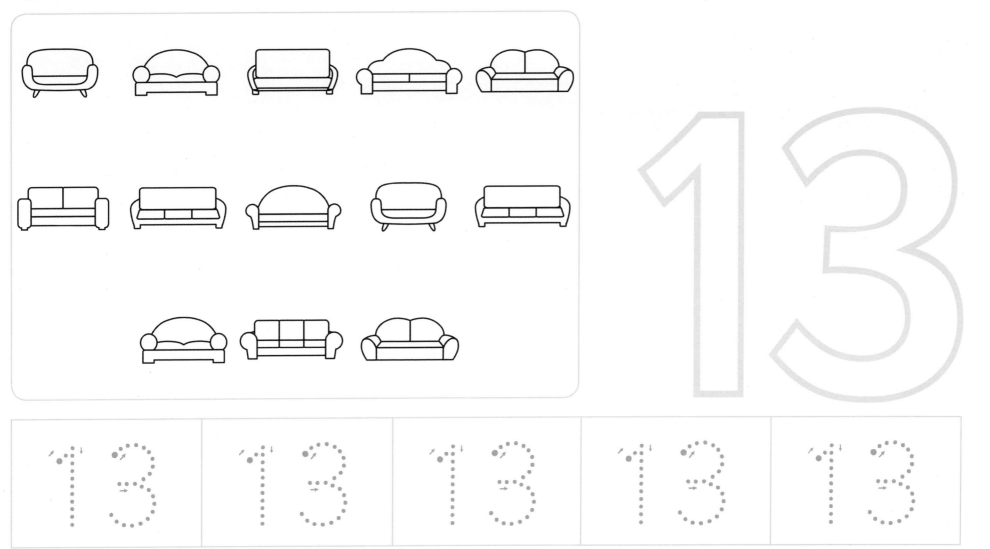

Presentation: Make a set of cards with thirteen objects we can find at home on each card (lamp, bed, fridge, sofa, shower). Show children a card. Ask: *What's this? How many [fridges] can you see?* Children count and say. Children open their books. They count the sofas and color in the number 13. Finally, children trace the number 13s.

Practice: Children sit in a circle. Give a child a ball. That child says *one* and passes the ball to the child next to him or her. That child says *two*, and so on. Children continue passing the ball until a child says *thirteen*. If they miss a number, they have to start all over again. Repeat as many times as you wish.

13

2¹₃ Count. ✏ Draw. ◯ Trace.

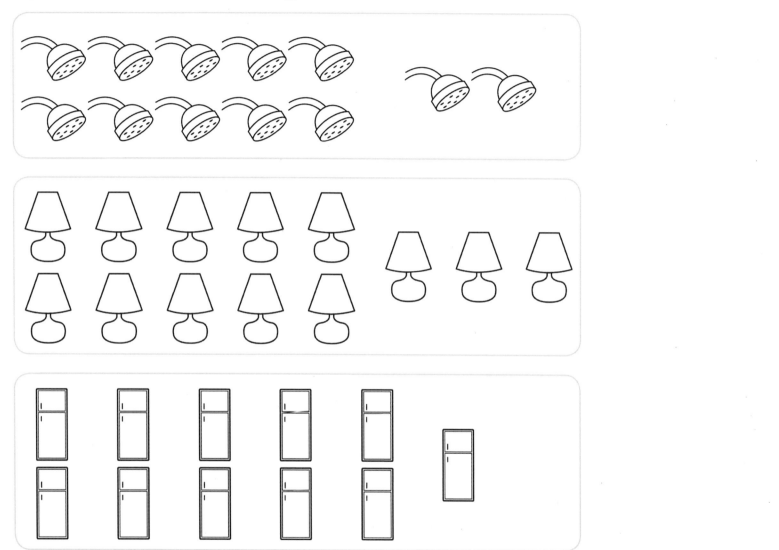

11 11

12

13

Presentation: Put the sets of cards with eleven, twelve, and thirteen objects we can find at home in a bag. Pull out a card and show it to children. Have them name and count the objects. Then lead children in writing the number in the air. Repeat as many times as you wish. Children open their books. Count the showers together with children. Have them draw a line from the showers to the number 12. Then they trace the number 12. Repeat this procedure with the remaining groups of objects and numbers.

Practice: Ask children to sit In small groups around a table or desk. Give each group a set of cards and a large piece of clay. Have them put the cards facedown on the table or desk. At the count of three, ask children to take a card, count the items, and form the correct number out of clay. The first group to finish wins. Repeat as many times as you wish.

4 Numbers 14 to 16

2$\frac{1}{3}$ Count. ✏ Color. ◯ Trace.

14

2$\frac{1}{3}$ Count. ✏ Color. ⬡ Trace.

Presentation: Make a set of cards with fifteen drawings of the same farm animal on each card (cow, duck, hen, sheep, horse, chick). Show children a card. Ask: *What's this? How many [horses] can you see?* Children count, say, and pretend to be [horses]. Children open their books. They count the ducks and color in the number 15. Finally, children trace the number 15s.

Practice: Children sit in a circle. Give a child a ball. That child says *one* and passes the ball to the child next to him or her. That child says *two*, and so on. Children continue passing the ball until a child says *fifteen*. If they miss a number, they have to start all over again. Repeat as many times as you wish.

2¹₃ Count. ✏ Color. ◯ Trace.

Presentation: *Make a set of cards with sixteen drawings of the same farm animal on each card (cow, duck, hen, sheep, horse, chick). Show children a card. Ask: What's this? How many [chicks] can you see? Children count, say, and pretend to be [chicks]. Children open their books. They count the sheep and color in the number 16. Finally, children trace the number 16s.*
Practice: *Arrange the cards facing the board. Invite a child to go to the board. The child turns over a card, counts the pictures, and writes the correct number below it. Repeat as many times as you wish.*

2⅓ Count. ✎ Write.

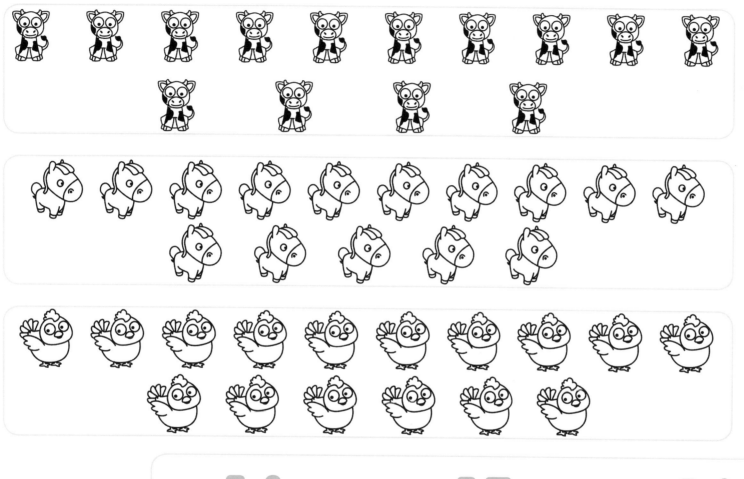

14   15   16

Presentation: Put the sets of cards with fourteen, fifteen, and sixteen farm animals in a bag. Pull out a card and show it to children. Have them name and count the animals. Then lead children in writing the number in the air. Repeat as many times as you wish. Children open their books. Count the cows together with children. Have them write the number 14 in on the line. Repeat this procedure with the remaining groups of farm animals and numbers. Encourage them to use the numbers at the bottom of the page as a model.

Practice: Ask children to sit in small groups around a table or desk. Give each group a set of cards and a large piece of clay. Have them put the cards facedown on the table or desk. On the count of three, ask children to take a card, count the items, and form the correct number out of clay. The first group to finish wins. Repeat as many times as you wish.

5 Numbers 17 to 19

2¹₃ Count. ✏ Color. ⬡ Trace.

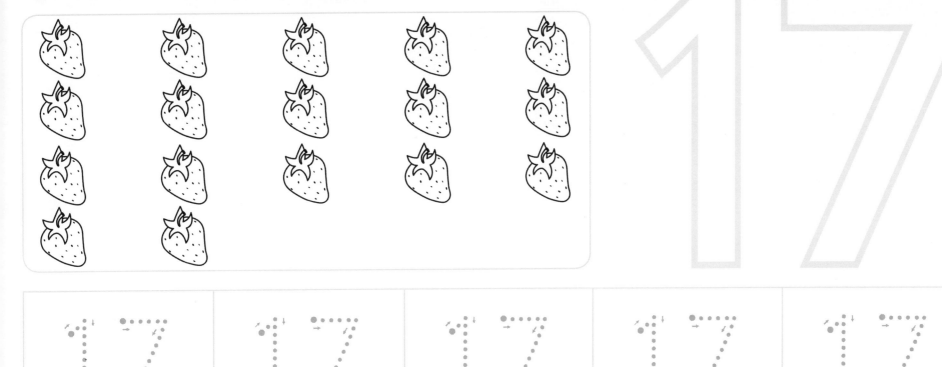

Presentation: Make a set of cards with seventeen drawings of the same food item on each card (strawberry, pancake, egg, carton of milk, box of juice, bottle of water). Show children a card. Ask: *What's this? How many [boxes of juice] can you see?* Children count and say. Lead children in drawing the number 17 in the air. Children open their books. They count the strawberries and color in the number 17. Finally, children trace the number 17s.
Practice: Give each child a large piece of play dough or clay. Say: *Make seventeen strawberries.* Children make and count the strawberries. Then they say: *Seventeen strawberries.*

19

2$\frac{1}{3}$ Count. ✏ Color. ⬭ Trace.

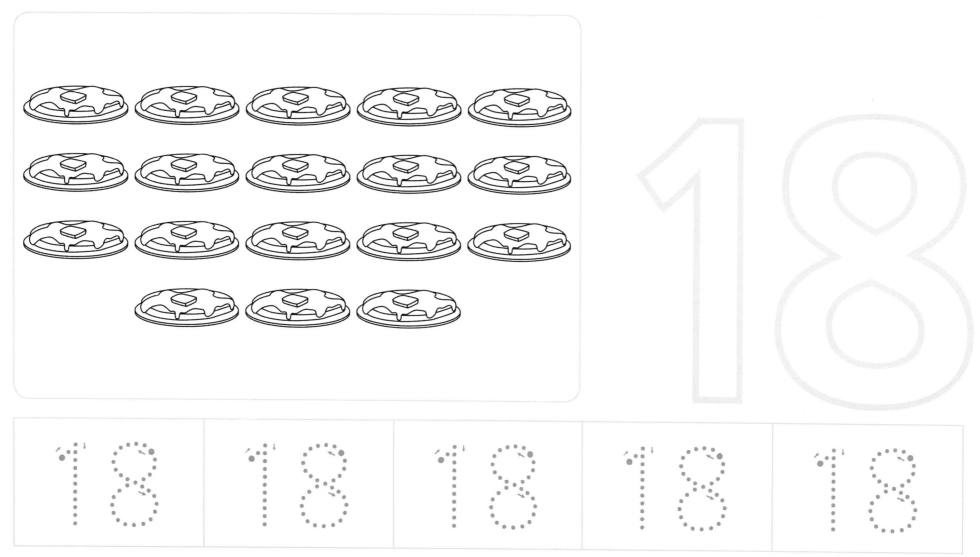

Presentation: Make a set of cards with eighteen drawings of the same food item on each card (strawberry, pancake, egg, carton of milk, box of juice, bottle of water). Show children a card. Ask: *What's this? How many [cartons of milk] can you see?* Children count and say. Lead children in drawing the number 18 in the air. Children open their books. They count the pancakes and color in the number 18. Finally, children trace the number 18s.

Practice: Display the cards around the classroom. Two children go to the back of the room. Say: *Find eighteen pancakes!* Children have to look for the correct card, attach it on the board, and write number 18 below it.

$2\frac{1}{3}$ Count. ✏ Color. ⭕ Trace.

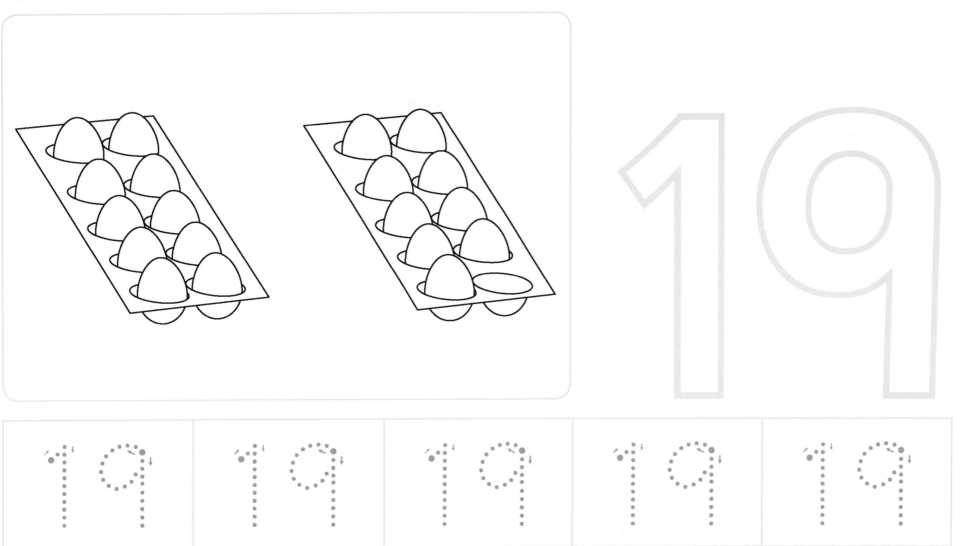

Presentation: Make a set of cards with nineteen drawings of the same food item on each card (strawberry, pancake, egg, carton of milk, box of juice, bottle of water). Show children a card. Ask: *What's this? How many [strawberries] can you see?* Children count and say. Lead children in drawing the number 19 in the air. Children open their books. They count the eggs and color in the number 19. Finally, children trace the number 19s.

Practice: Children sit in a circle. Give a child a ball. That child says *one* and passes the ball to the child next to him or her. That child says *two*, and so on. Children continue passing the ball until a child says *nineteen*. If they miss a number, they have to start all over again. Repeat as many times as you wish.

 Say. 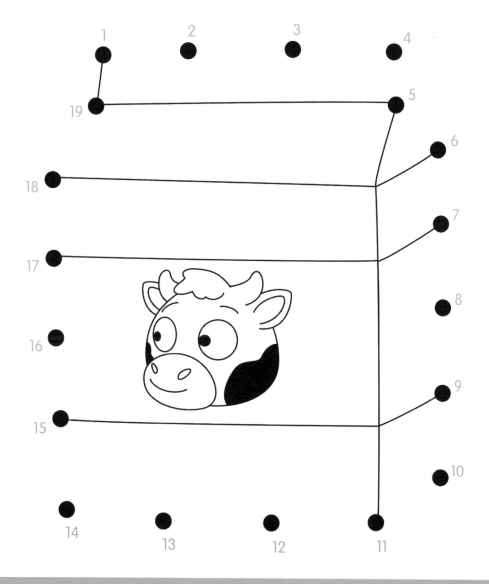 Draw.

Presentation: Put the sets of cards with seventeen, eighteen, and nineteen food items in a bag. Pull out a card and show it to children. Have them name and count the food items. Then lead children in writing the number in the air. Repeat as many times as you wish. Children open their books. They point to each number and say it aloud. Children connect the dots as they say each number. Ask: *What is it?*

Practice: Arrange the cards facing the board. Invite a child to go to the board. The child turns over a card, counts the pictures, and writes the correct number below it. Repeat as many times as you wish.

6 Numbers 1 to 20

2¹₃ Count. ✏ Color. ⬭ Trace.

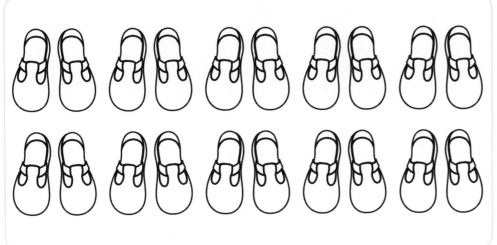

20

Presentation: Make a set of cards with twenty drawings of the same clothing item on each card (pants, shoe, sock, T-shirt, sweater, dress, skirt, jacket, boot, raincoat). Show children a card. Ask: *What's this? How many [skirts] can you see?* Children count and say. Lead children in drawing the number 20 in the air. Children open their books. They count the shoes and color in the number 20. Finally, children trace the number 20s.
Practice: Give each child a large piece of play dough or clay. Children form the number 20 and then they say: *Twenty.*

2¹₃ Count. ✏ Color.

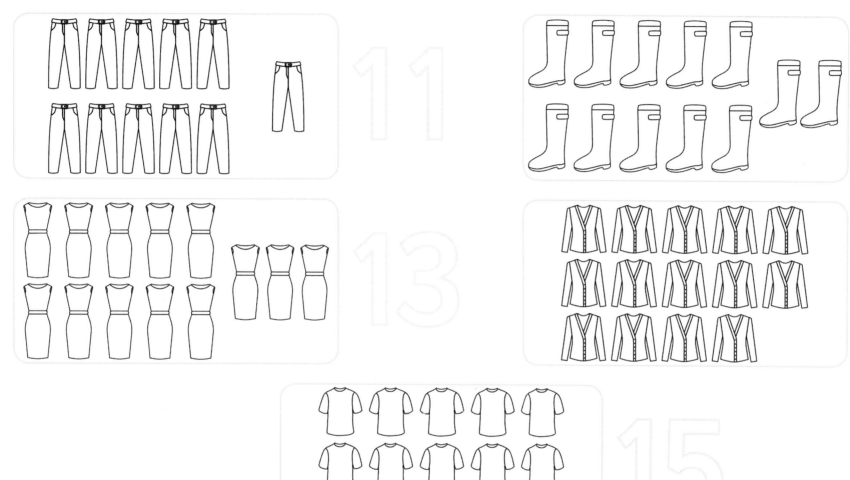

Presentation: Make a set of cards with eleven to fifteen of the same clothing item on each card (pants, shoe, sock, T-shirt, sweater, dress, skirt, jacket, boot, raincoat). Show children a card. Ask: *What's this? How many [raincoats] can you see?* Children count and say. Children open their books. Count the pairs of pants together with children. Then have them color in the number 11. Repeat this procedure with the remaining groups of clothing items and numbers.

Practice: Display the cards around the classroom. Divide the class into two teams. A child from each team goes to the back of the classroom. Say: *Find a card with eleven pictures!* Children find a card with eleven clothing items, attach it to the board, and write the correct number below it. If they do it correctly, they win a point for their team. The team with the most points wins the game.

2¹₃ Count. ◯ Trace.

 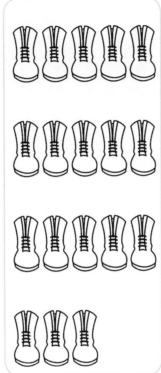 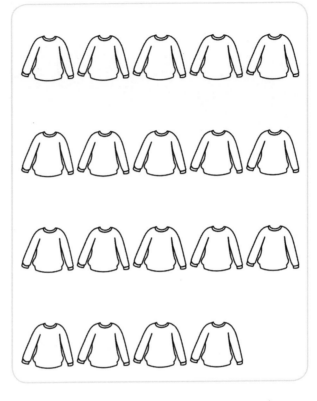 

25

2⅓ Count. 👆 Point. ✏ Write.

Presentation: Divide the class into small groups. Make a set of cards with numbers 1 to 20 for each group. Have children put the numbers in the correct order. Then have them count as they point to each number card. Children open their books. They count to twenty while pointing to the correct spaces on the page. Finally, have them write the missing numbers to complete the sequence.

Practice: Put various number cards between 1 and 20 in a bag. Draw twenty circles on the board and display the remaining cards in the circles, in their correct sequential position. Play some music and have children pass around the bag. Stop the music. The child with the bag pulls out a card, says the number, and attaches it in the correct circle. Once children have completed the sequence, lead them in counting to twenty as you point to each number on the board.

Numbers 21 to 30

2¹₃ Count. ✏ Color.

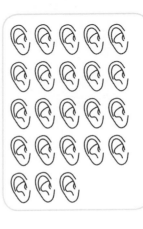

Presentation: Make a set of cards with twenty-one to twenty-five of the same body parts we use for our senses on each card (eye, hand, ear, nose, mouth). Show children a card. Ask: *What's this? How many [noses] can you see?* Children count and say. Children open their books and count the eyes with you. Then have them color in the number 21. Repeat this procedure with the remaining groups of body parts and numbers.

Practice: Write the numbers 21 to 25 on the board, but out of order. Invite a child to the board and have him or her choose a card. The child looks at the card, counts the pictures, and attaches the card to the board under the correct number. Repeat as many times as you wish.

27

2⅓ Count. ✏ Color.

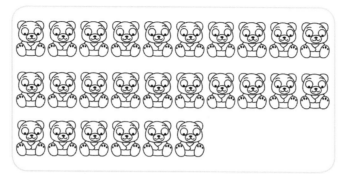

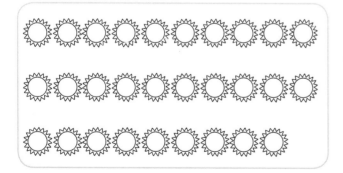

Presentation: Make a set of cards with twenty-six to thirty of the same item that children can see, smell, touch, hear, or taste on each card (butterfly, flower, cat, singing bird, apple). Show children a card. Ask: *What's this? How many [birds] can you see?* Children count and say. Children open their books and count the teddy bears with you. Then have them color in the number 26. Repeat this procedure with the remaining items and numbers.

28

Practice: Write the numbers 26 to 30 on the board. Put the cards in a bag. Play some music and have children pass around the bag. Stop the music. The child with the bag pulls out a card, counts the pictures, and attaches it below the correct number on the board.

2¹₃ Count. ○ Circle.

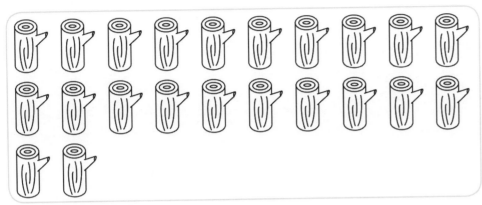

21   22   23

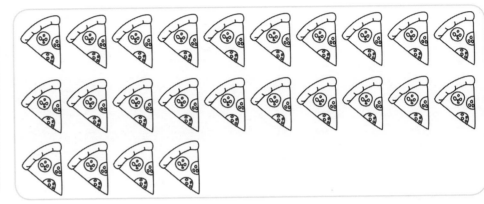

24   25   26

26   27   28

28   29   30

Presentation: Make a set of cards with twenty-one to thirty of the same item that children can see, smell, touch, hear, or taste on each card (sunset, cut orange, stuffed animal, siren, pear). Show children a card. Ask: *What's this? How many [sirens] can you see?* Children count and say. Children open their books and count the logs with you. Then they circle the number 22. Repeat this procedure with the remaining items and numbers.
Practice: Children sit in a circle. Give a child a ball. That child says *one* and passes the ball to the child next to him or her. That child says *two*, and so on. Children continue passing the ball until a child says *thirty*. If they miss a number, they have to start all over again. Repeat as many times as you wish.

29

2¹⁄₃ Count. 👆 Point. ✏ Write.

Presentation: Divide the class into small groups. Make a set of cards with numbers 1 to 30 for each group. Have children put the numbers in the correct order. Then have them count as they point to each number card. Children open their books. Ask them to count to 30 while pointing to the correct spaces on the page. Finally, have them write the missing numbers to complete the sequence.

Practice: Put various number cards between 1 and 30 in a bag. Draw thirty squares on the board and display the remaining cards in the squares in their correct sequential position. Play some music and have children pass around the bag. Stop the music. The child with the bag pulls out a card, says the number, and attaches it in the correct square. Once children have completed the sequence, lead them in counting to thirty as you point to each number on the board.

8 Numbers 31 to 40

$2\frac{1}{3}$ Count. ✏ Color.

31

32

33

34

35

Presentation: Make a set of cards with thirty-one to thirty-five drawings of an object we use for transportation on each card (car, boat, ship, bus, train, plane, bike, helicopter). Show children a card. Ask: *What's this? How many [bikes] can you see?* Children count and say. Children open their books and count the cars with you. Then have them color in the number 31. Repeat this procedure with the remaining groups of objects and numbers.

Practice: Write the numbers 31 to 35 on the board but out of order. Invite a child to the board and have him or her choose a card. The child looks at the card, counts the pictures, and attaches the card to the board under the correct number. Repeat as many times as you wish.

2⅓ Count. ✏ Color.

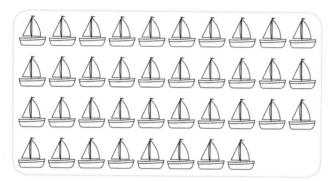

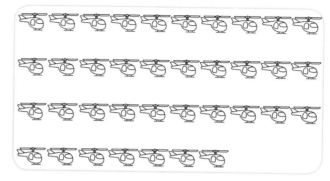

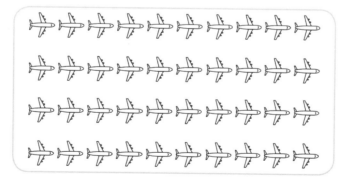

36   37   38   39   40

Presentation: Make a set of cards with thirty-six to forty drawings of an object we use for transportation on each card (car, boat, ship, bus, train, plane, bike, helicopter). Show children a card. Ask: *What's this? How many [cars] can you see?* Children count and say. Children open their books and count the bikes with you. Then they color in the number 36. Repeat this procedure with the remaining groups of objects and numbers.

Practice: Display the cards around the classroom. Divide the class into two teams. A child from each team goes to the back of the classroom. Say: *Find a card with thirty-seven objects!* Children find a card with thirty-seven objects, attach it to the board, and write the correct number below it. If they do it correctly, they win a point for their team. The team with the most points wins the game.

2⅓ Count. ◯ Trace. ✏ Write.

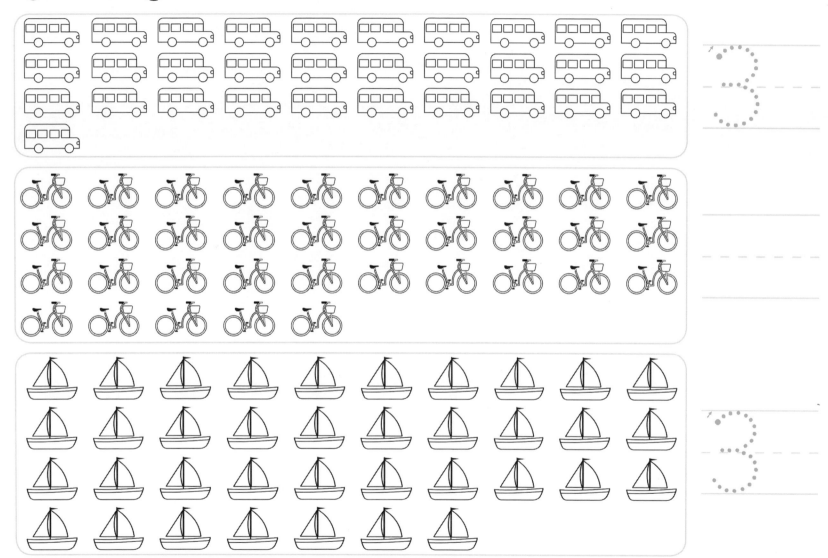

Presentation: Make a set of cards with thirty-one to forty drawings of an object we use for transportation on each card (car, boat, ship, bus, train, plane, bike, helicopter). Show children a card. Ask: *What's this? How many [boats] can you see?* Children count and say. Children open their books and count the buses with you. Then they trace the number 3 and write the number 1 to complete the number 31. Repeat this procedure with the remaining groups of objects and numbers.

Practice: Children sit in a circle. Give a child a ball. That child says *one* and passes the ball to the child next to him or her. That child says *two*, and so on. Children continue passing the ball until a child says *forty*. If they miss a number, they have to start all over again. Repeat as many times as you wish.

$2\frac{1}{3}$ Count. 👆 Point. ✏️ Write.

Presentation: Divide the class into small groups. Make a set of cards with the numbers 1 to 40 for each group. Have children put the numbers in the correct order. Then have them count as they point to each number card. Children open their books. Ask them to count to forty while pointing to the correct spaces on the page. Finally, have them write the missing numbers to complete the sequence.

Practice: Divide the class into small groups. Give each group a large piece of play dough or clay. Say: *Make a train with forty train cars.* Children work together to form a train with forty train cars. Then they count the train cars together.

9 Numbers 41 to 50

2$\frac{1}{3}$ Count. ✏ Color.

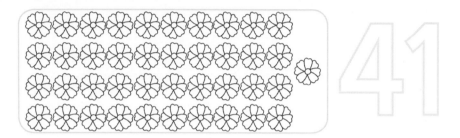

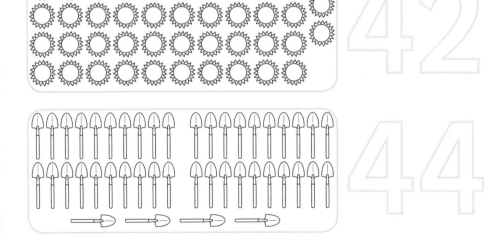

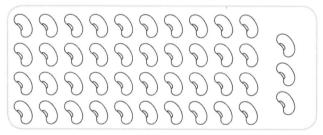

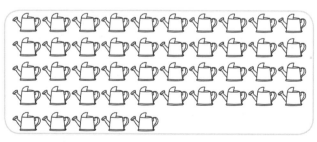

Presentation: Make a set of cards with forty-one to forty-five drawings of an item related to plants on each card (plant, flower, sun, seed, shovel, watering can). Show children a card. Ask: *What's this? How many [suns] can you see?* Children count and say. Children open their books and count the flowers with you. Then have them color in the number 41. Repeat this procedure with the remaining groups of objects and numbers.

Practice: Display the cards around the classroom. Play some music and encourage children to dance to the rhythm. Stop the music. Say: *Touch a card with forty-three items!* Children touch a card with forty-three items. Repeat with other numbers.

2$\frac{1}{3}$ Count. ✏ Color.

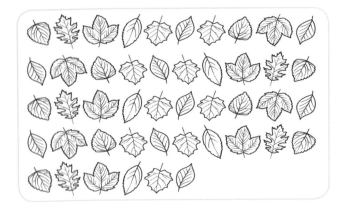

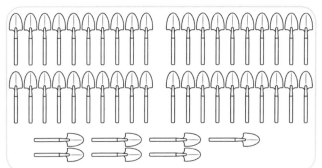

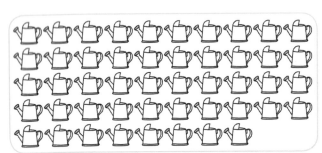

Presentation: Make a set of cards with forty-six to fifty drawings of an item related to plants on each card (plant, flower, sun, seed, shovel, watering can). Show children a card. Ask: *What's this? How many [seeds] can you see?* Children count and say. Children open their books and count the leaves with you. Then have them color in the number 46. Repeat this procedure with the remaining groups of objects and numbers.

Practice: Display the cards around the classroom. Divide the class into two teams. A child from each team goes to the back of the classroom. Say: *Find a card with forty-nine objects!* Children find a card with forty-nine objects, attach it to the board, and write the correct number below it. If they do it correctly, they win a point for their team. The team with the most points wins the game.

👁 Look. 2¹₃ Count. ✏ Color.

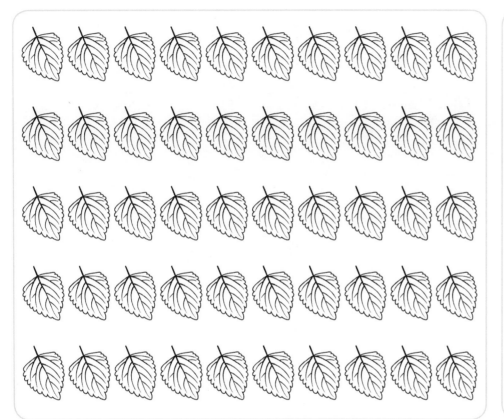

41

47

Presentation: Make a set of cards with forty-one to fifty drawings of an item related to plants on each card (plant, flower, sun, seed, shovel, watering can). Show children a card. Ask: *What's this? How many [shovels] can you see?* Children count and say. Children open their books. With children, look at the first number and lead them in counting the correct number of leaves. Then have them color in forty-one leaves. Repeat with the remaining number.

Practice: Children sit in a circle. Give a child a ball. That child says *one* and passes the ball to the child next to him or her. That child says *two*, and so on. Children continue passing the ball until a child says *fifty*. If they miss a number, they have to start all over again. Repeat as many times as you wish.

 Say. Draw.

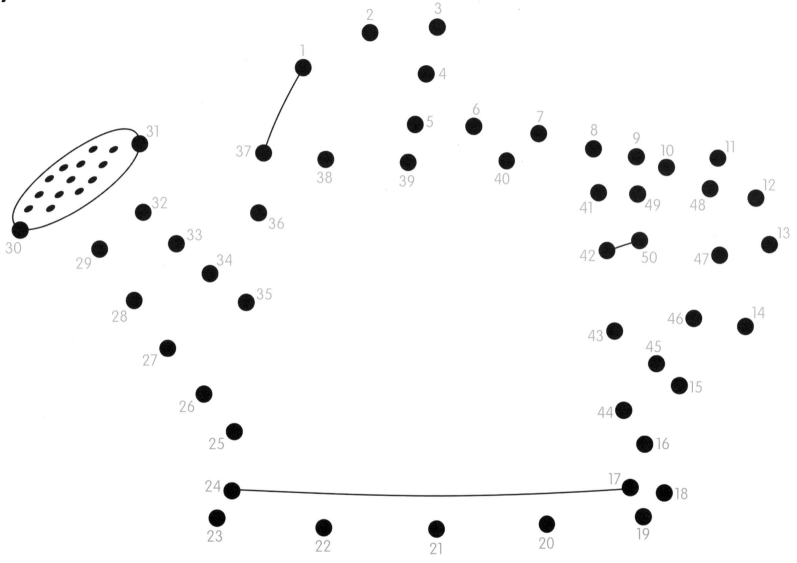

Presentation: Divide the class into small groups. Make a set of cards with the numbers 1 to 50 for each group. Have children put the numbers in the correct order. Then have them count as they point to each number card. Children open their books. They point to each number and say it aloud. Children connect the dots as they say each number. Ask: *What is it?*

Practice: Put various number cards between 1 and 50 in a bag. Draw fifty rectangles on the board and display the remaining cards in the rectangles in their correct sequential position. Play some music and have children pass around the bag. Stop the music. The child with the bag pulls out a card, says the number, and attach it in the correct rectangle. Once children have completed the sequence, lead them in counting to fifty as you point to each number on the board.

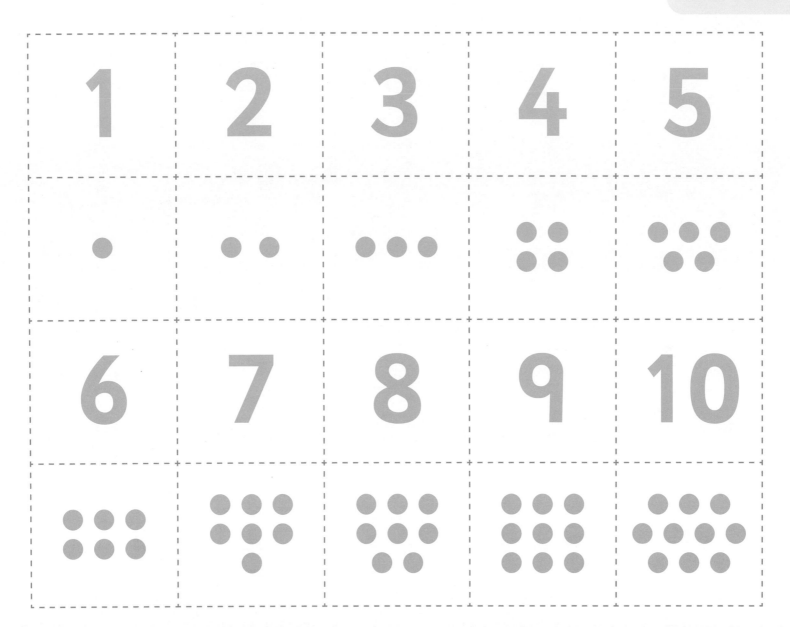

Have children cut out the memory cards and put each set in an envelope or a small bag. Have children sit in pairs. Ask children to mix up the cards and put them facedown on a table or desk. Then, alternating, they turn over any two cards. If they find a pair, they take it. The child with the most pairs wins. You can also have children play *Slap!* by asking them to sit in small groups around a table or desk and put the cards faceup. Call out a number. The first child to slap the correct card keeps it. The child with the most cards in each team wins the game.